FORAGING

Joy Howard

ARACHNE PRESS

First published in UK 2017 by Arachne Press Limited
100 Grierson Road, London SE23 1NX
www.arachnepress.com
© Joy Howard 2017
 ISBN: 978-1-909208-39-1

Text decorations ©Nikser, Shutterstock

Printed on wood-free paper in the UK by TJ International, Padstow.

FORAGING

Acknowledgements

These poems or versions of them have appeared in the following magazines and anthologies.

'fiat lux' *Orbis*; 'A Perfect Hexagon' *The Price of Gold* (Grey Hen Press 2012); 'Empty' *The Book of Love and Loss* (Belgrave Press 2014); 'Fernsehen' *Slants of Light* (Paragram Poetry Prize 2013) and *Fanfare* (Second Light Publications 2015); 'Out to Lunch' *Orbis*; 'Going Back' and 'Stranded' *Running Before the Wind* (Grey Hen Press 2013); 'Hydro' *The Frogmore Papers*; 'vita brevis' *Wenlock Festival Anthology* (Fair Acre Press 2015).

CONTENTS

Constellation	7
At the Window, Waiting	8
Melangell and the Hare	10
Endgame	12
Lineage	13
fiat lux	14
In Clover	16
Jubilee	18
A Perfect Hexagon	19
Armadillo	20
Empty	21
Fernsehen	22
Magnetic	23
Houses for the Working Man	24
Blank Document	26
Olympus Inc.	28
Out to Lunch	30
Red Frock, Green Frock	31
Hydro	32
Living to Tell the Tale	33
vita brevis	34
Foraging	35
January	36
The Reach	37
Stranded	38
Morning	39
Terroir	40
Going Back	41

Constellation
For Barbara, a retrospective

Draco appears over the horizon
flashing her diamonds
the usual display

her brightness   her talents
her ancient and present splendour

Enter the dragon
dazzlement
trust it

At the Window, Waiting
Hammershøi / Friedrich

She stands
owned by a locked landscape
snow trees mist

The stillness of eternity

She dreams
a green frock an open window
a crowding of ship's masts

The expectation of love

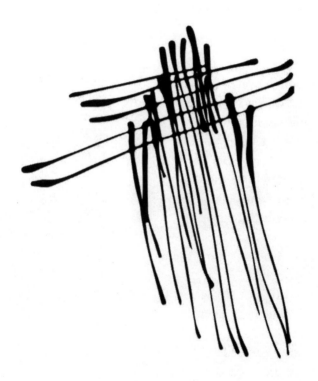

Melangell and the Hare

Small she was so when it
came to it
there was no difficulty being
a hare

when she leapt she could see
as high over
the wall as when she had
human legs

so leapt and saw low sun
picking out
spear points and angry eyes
hounds coursing

in a woman's skirts she hid
invincible
no dog would near her
and the hunt knelt

run on hare's legs she had
over the water
from compliance and hand-fasting
to live husbandless

now bargains were made
and peace promised
the gift of the valley settled her
as rain lays dust

led her to her end of days
many-seasoned
to lie at the last in her chapel
true to her stone form

The mediæval church at Pennant Melangell with its shrine containing the
bones of the seventh century St Melangell has attracted visitors and pilgrims
from all over the world. Melangell is the patron saint of hares, rabbits and
small animals.

Endgame

A thin wisp of woodsmoke
catches the throat

foxes are barking the dawn in
soon comes a cold sun.

A last day should be gold
and gentle with blackberries

but ice claws at the window:
it has begun.

Lineage

When a harrow turns the sod
and dark earth creams over
in a slow wave-curl
what we hope to glimpse
is the dulled gold of a ring.

No coin, no cup handle
no brooch nor jewelled cloak pin
surrenders to this ancient instinct –
the slipping on to the finger
the twisting round, the here and now
of ring-giver, ring-gifted
the circling of time beneath the plough.

fiat lux

in our darkness
we have need of you

illuminate our dull days
with slantways sun-glimmer
warm us with flame

flood our slow minds
with enlightenment
brighten us with hope

widen our eyes to truth
torch our imaginings
set us free

The old Celtic bards used to go into special dark houses and stay there
until they had worked out their poems.

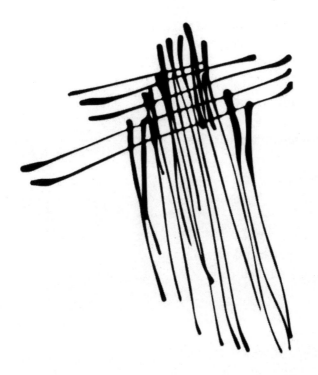

In Clover

Wonder if wandering to the far field
                    would find
a mouthful kinder on the gums
               softer on
the stomachs

But risk my hide on the barbs
                      the mud slip
face the unfamiliar eyes
                 of sheep?
some other day maybe some
                       other day

Chew chew chew
    burdock and plantain
sanfoin and chicory
                chew chew chew

What
's this   smells
like raindrops
             tastes
like calf's breath
             feels
like a soft wet
    muzzle nuzzle

Not leaving now no way
roll me over brothers
and sisters this
is it   found my purple
patch

paradise

Jubilee

Day after grey day rain follows rain –
flags droop in mizzle
display swirls down drains

But now see the sun come
hunting the rain down –
gardens are fanfares
lawns a strewing of petals
clotheslines
a sudden explosion of bunting

A Perfect Hexagon

It's to the bees' advantage
that the shape providing
the maximum cell area
has the minimum expenditure
of energy and materials.

And engineers confirm
that such a structure provides
the maximum strength –
at 0.05mm thick each wall
supports 25 times
its own weight.

But mathematicians
still conjecture
that as the cell bottom consists
of 3 equal rhombi
there's an isoperimetric
problem for honeycombs -
close to but not quite
the optimal.

Let's hope the bees are working on this.
Time is running out.

Armadillo

With your sharp-visored face and silvered ear-guards
you move as fast as your too-small war boots will allow
feeling the slow drag of your armoured tail.

Such accomplished knighthood looks out of place
under the cloud canopy. This rainy marching will rust you.
Your plates, inflexible at best, will lose their curl.

At Agincourt you'd at least have had the backing of the longbows
and the services of a decent armourer to fix your rivets
if not the sixteen hours sleep you need before each foray.

Improbably, news is you are tops in the battle for survival. You
and your nine-banded brothers are taking no prisoners
in the rain forest. It's your Pink Fairy cousins yielding the day.

Population numbers of nearly all armadillo species are threatened by habitat
loss and over-hunting. Only the nine-band population is expanding, and
some species, including the Pink Fairy, are threatened.

Empty

Houses need to be lived in –
yours, empty for a year,
is showing its displeasure.

Wallpaper droops
from the ceiling – a dozen
small flies in cobweb shrouds
shadow windows.

There's not much dust
no living thing to feed it –
likewise the dehumidifier
no longer whirrs.

Detritus, still unsorted
reproachful of the hand
that has stopped clearing
lies in unchanging heaps.

My hand, your house
both missing you.
Emptiness.

Fernsehen

All the colours and the conflicts
of the world are in my sight
but a corner of my eye escapes the glare

catches a glim of gold-dust flight
climbing the penlight slide of sun
piercing the curtain shield

a small invader prone to do great harm
whose hatchlings threaten
my cashmere my best velvet

and I should clap it in my hands
finish its glittering dance
along the dusty sword of light

but am entranced
released from wars of attrition
far and near

Fernsehen – to watch television: literally 'seeing far'

Magnetic

'A needle in the mind' *Migrants* RS Thomas

Your true north
is a complex deity

but it's a simple line
of black on white
that swivels me

inevitable as iron

Houses for the Working Man
Town Council records, Bangor 1896

We are agreed

no shop, store or warehouse no laundry

no bathrooms no lodgers

no shed no greenhouse or fowlhouse

no fowls

no pigeons or other animals
apart from cats

We are disappointed

not many tenants

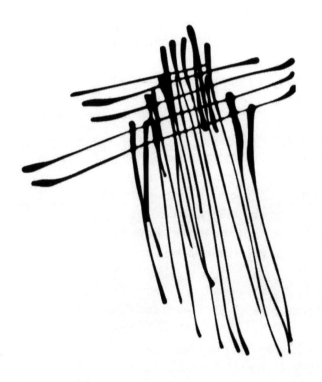

Blank Document

A poet pours out words like a river –
beautiful sonorous freewheeling words
transfiguring the mundane
with ease and charm.
She tells us about her love of poems
and adds that she doesn't like admin.

One day when words won't come
consider this.

While the creative genie can pack up
her bags and disappear at the drop
of her delightful hat, leaving you in need
of a stout shoulder to lean on, there she is,
dear old reliable relative, ready
to fill your empty hours with purpose
and a sense of solid achievement.

The baleful white stare of the empty screen
holds no fears for her. Create a table, she croons,
lay it out in columns, rows, small boxes.
Fill with essential information.
Arrange in folders. Colour-code.
Repeat as often as necessary.
Suggestions for entry include bills
receipts (with dates), to-dos, have-dones,
orders made and filled, lists about
almost everything.

Meanwhile stash all your old love letters
and poems in an old-fashioned filing cabinet.
You can sort those out later.

Olympus Inc.

We're a long-established
family-run outfit specialising
in sorting out your poetry problems.
Get yourself published and win
that prestigious competition!

We love anything classical
and our mum, Hera
is particularly good on how to go about
working on a long sequence – click
on '*Scaffolding*'.

The boys are always up for
sorting you out with
a good title: see '*Roof*'.
For general editing it's '*Gutter*'
run by head honcho, Zeus.

If you're interested in exploring
new forms, our youngest is the ideas man:
why not try his '*Tree*'?
And the daughter has expertise in owls,
spiders and nature poetry in general.

A disclaimer: we make no claims
promises or guarantees about the accuracy
completeness or adequacy of
prognoses emanating from Delphi.

Out to Lunch

the way a poet
will pick up the book you hand her
and disappear

in the middle of a conversation
away she goes and you know
you're talking to yourself

rinsed clean by the immersion
she'll resume engagement
with the world and you

but something's changed
her ear's half listening
tuned to a remote frequency

you could get her to agree
that trip to the Hebrides
she'd hear it as Hesperides

where lunch beneath
the dappled shade
would be golden apples

Red Frock, Green Frock

for my sister

Two little girlies walking down the street
satchels on backs, sandals on feet.

Words thrown sideways shatter like glass
teardrops gather, splatter on grass.

Poor little girlies, now it's blood and guts
taunting, tearing, bruises, cuts.

Fifty years is what it takes to close the can of worms
hug each other, kiss each other, come to terms.

Hydro

at breakfast in the restaurant
the waitress does a slow Strathspey
around the cluttered tables
and he's giving it some on his mobile

the lady weekenders stare down
at the oatcakes and crowdie
then take up their bickering
golf versus shopping (no clear winner)

he doesn't notice the fine emanation
of disapproval encircling him like
a cloud of Highland midges
though he scratches his hair as they pass

at tea there will be a discussion
skewered by Cairngorm
on the relative merits of tee-offs and twinsets
while out in the foyer he'll still be full on

no-one will be talking about colonic irrigation

Living to Tell the Tale

I sit and look at him

He's handsome   sure enough
and so I thought when I first saw him
eyeing me up *chez nous*   but now
his is the face of death

Talk your way out of this one
Shahrazad

If I can't   I'm dead
and that's a thought
to kill off flights of fancy
if ever I heard one

I'm beyond terrified
but I've got to give it a try
so through a fog of fear   off I go
and I make it   this time

Soon enough I'm on a roll
I amaze myself.
I'm keeping my head
sure enough

They tell me it's over
murder has left his face
so all I have to do now
is not throw up when he fucks me

over and over and over

vita brevis

Her horny hands unpick the seams of the day
to let in evening. She works away at it
the old hag of the mountains.

When it's dark she scatters
trinkets – bling for the tourists
gewgaws spilled from her silver dish –
she laughs as they lap it up.

One visit and they think they know the place
promise each other they'll be back –
but no: one life is all they've got.
One go at discovering what's on offer.

It's not a rehearsal.

Foraging

The bees are working the cotoneaster.
What are they finding there? The blossom's gone
small berries green, not yet plumped and reddened
for autumn birds.

The spikes of lavender are grey and upright
but soon there'll be the purpling up, the swaying
in the wind, the bending with the weight of bees
in a stream of sunlight.

And you'd be basking on your bench
loving the busyness: bees in the blooms
me cutting back the shrubbery. You motionless
as a Henry Moore.

Or dancing on the lawn, loving life and the roses –
bright as July till paths defeat you and grass
turns treacherous. So begins the bringing of small posies
daily to your door.

The last of these a February one and took some doing
among the wintry shrubs and scrub of moss and leaves
under cold skies. Mourning weather. I laid it with slow care
upon your coffin.

And I've still not told the bees.

January

wolf-month
food is scarce

menaced by hungrier
than us and fiercer
moon shadows loom

open gates
give tithe

live with wolf

The Reach

September

There are swans homing in
for the willows

and the reed-rocking wake
of their progress over the water

laps at the margins
of this gentlest of summers

December

It's dark the river's flooding
some have drowned

never second-guess
a year's end

Stranded

and anchored in a fretwork of foam
over sea-shimmering silver gilt sand
I'm bliss-basking like an old grey seal
beached and loving it

so till the seventh wave
lolls over me and nudges me back
to the sea let your hands glide
over mounded flesh and soft pelt
while you plumb my fathomable eyes
and marvel at my stillness

believe me
I'm more graceful in water

Morning

Waking to you sleeping at my side
a shoulder cool for kissing
slope of back warm for smoothing by a hand
the dark V at your nape spearing my heart –
or facing me, unheeding of my gaze
your closed eyes busy with dreaming –
is the time I love you most;
your body as a garment
thrown lightly on a chair-back:
abandoned, soft, sweet-smelling,
awaiting the inhabitation of the day.

Terroir

Beneath this thin and dusty soil
where I try to coax growth
from straggling seedlings
there is constant welling
and rock.

Water carves rock
but rock binds water
releases springs and falls
wild courses constrained
to river and lake.

Love is sunlit
playful, flooding
but it's bedrock
that forms *terroir* –
sustaining, defining
constant in dry seasons.

Going Back

Shore turf tugs at the old boat
a slow careful pulling in
grass and wild flowers
spread through the ribs
prow and stern only mind-held
salt bleached shape lines

The sea comes in for you
swirls through the sand pools
each small wave-scour
gentling you out with the tide

In this place you stay with me
shaped by the sea that you loved
and the tide is that same tide
which will come for all of us

ABOUT THE AUTHOR

Joy Howard founded Grey Hen Press, specialising in publishing the work of older women poets, post retirement in 2007. With seven Grey Hen Press anthologies, a chapbook series, and the new imprint Hen Run under her belt, she's now in her mid-seventies but still waiting to run out of steam.

Joy is widely published in anthologies, magazines and journals, and online.

Collections:

Exit Moonshine (Grey Hen 2009),

Refurbishment (Ward Wood 2011).

ABOUT ARACHNE PRESS
www.arachnepress.com

Arachne Press is a micro publisher of (award-winning!) short story and poetry anthologies and collections, novels including a Carnegie Medal nominated young adult novel, and a photographic portrait collection. We are very grateful to Arts Council England for financial support for this book and three others, a tour round the UK and our live events.

We are expanding our range all the time, but the short form is our first love. We keep fiction and poetry live, through readings, festivals, our regular event The Story Sessions, workshops, exhibitions and all things to do with writing.

Follow us on Twitter:
@ArachnePress
@SolShorts

Like us on Facebook:
ArachnePress
SolsticeShorts2014
TheStorySessions

BOOKS

OUT NOW:

With Paper for Feet by Jennifer A McGowan
ISBN: 978-1-909208-35-3
Poetry exploring myth and folklore
COMING APRIL 2017:
Happy Ending NOT Guaranteed by Liam Hogan
ISBN: 978-1-909208-36-0
Deliciously twisted fantasy stories.

BACK LIST:
Short Stories
London Lies
ISBN: 978-1-909208-00-1
Our first Liars' League showcase, featuring unlikely tales set in London.
Stations: Short Stories Inspired by the Overground line
ISBN: 978-1-909208-01-8
A story for every station from New Cross, Crystal Palace, and West Croydon at the Southern extremes of the East London branch of the Overground line, all the way to Highbury & Islington.
Lovers' Lies
ISBN: 978-1-909208-02-5
Our second collaboration with Liars' League, bringing the freshness, wit, imagination and passion of their authors to stories of love.
Weird Lies
ISBN: 978-1-909208-10-0
WINNER of the Saboteur2014 Best Anthology Award: our third Liars' League collaboration – more than twenty stories

varying in style from tales not out of place in *One Thousand and One Nights* to the completely bemusing.

Solstice Shorts: Sixteen Stories about Time
ISBN: 978-1-909208-23-0
Winning stories from the first *Solstice Shorts Festival* competition together with a story from each of the competition judges.

Mosaic of Air by Cherry Potts
ISBN: 978-1-909208-03-2
Sixteen short stories from a lesbian perspective.

Liberty Tales, Stories & Poems inspired by Magna Carta edited by Cherry Potts
ISBN: 978-1-909208-31-5
Because freedom is never out of fashion.

Shortest Day, Longest Night
ISBN: 978-1-909208-28-5
Stories and poems from the *Solstice Shorts Festival* 2015 and 2016.

Poetry

The Other Side of Sleep: Narrative Poems
ISBN: 978-1-909208-18-6
Long, narrative poems by contemporary voices, including Inua Elams, Brian Johnstone, and Kate Foley, whose title poem for the anthology was the winner of the 2014 *Second Light* Long Poem competition.

The Don't Touch Garden by Kate Foley
ISBN: 978-1-909208-19-3
A complex autobiographical collection of poems of adoption and identity, from award-winning poet Kate Foley.

Novels

Devilskein & Dearlove by Alex Smith
ISBN: 978-1-909208-15-5
NOMINATED FOR THE 2015 CILIP CARNEGIE
MEDAL.
A young adult novel set in South Africa. Young Erin Dearlove
has lost everything, and is living in a run-down apartment
block in Cape Town. Then she has tea with Mr Devilskein,
the demon who lives on the top floor, and opens a door into
another world.
The Dowry Blade by Cherry Potts
ISBN: 979-1-909208-20-9
When nomad Brede finds a wounded mercenary and the
Dowry Blade, she is set on a journey of revenge, love, and loss.

Photography

Outcome: LGBT Portraits by Tom Dingley
ISBN: 978-1-909208-26-1
80 full colour photographic portraits of LGBT people
with the attributes of their daily life – and a photograph of
themselves as a child. @OutcomeLGBT

All our books (except Poetry titles) are also available as
e-books.

EVENTS

Arachne Press is enthusiastic about live literature and we make an effort to present our books through readings.

The Solstice Shorts Festival

(http://arachnepress.com/solstice-shorts)

Now in its third year, Solstice Shorts is all about time: held on the shortest day of the year on the Prime meridian, stories, poetry and song celebrate the turning of the moon, the changing of the seasons, the motions of the spheres, and clockwork!

We showcase our work and that of others at our own bi-monthly live literature event, in south London: *The Story Sessions,* which we run like a folk club, with headliners and opportunities for the audience to join in (http://arachnepress.com/the-story-sessions)

We are always on the lookout for other places to show off, so if you run a bookshop, a literature festival or any other kind of literature venue, get in touch; we'd love to talk to you.

WORKSHOPS

We offer writing workshops suitable for writers' groups, literature festivals and evening classes, which are sometimes supported by live music – if you are interested, please get in touch.